EASIEST
KEYBOARD
COLLECTION

Smash Hits

WISE PUBLICATIONS
London/New York/Paris/Sydney/Copenhagen/Madrid/Tokyo

Exclusive Distributors:

Music Sales Limited
8/9 Frith Street,
London W1V 5TZ, England.

Music Sales Pty Limited
120 Rothschild Avenue,
Rosebery, NSW 2018,
Australia.

Order No. AM963875
ISBN 0-7119-8146-9
This book © Copyright 2000 by Wise Publications

Compiled by Nick Crispin
Music arranged by Roger Day
Music processed by Paul Ewers Music Design

Printed in the United Kingdom by
Caligraving Limited, Thetford, Norfolk.

Cover photograph (Robbie Williams) courtesy of
London Features International.

Your Guarantee of Quality
As publishers, we strive to produce every book to the highest
commercial standards.
The music has been freshly engraved and the book has been carefully
designed to minimise awkward page turns and to make playing from
it a real pleasure.
Particular care has been given to specifying acid-free, neutral-sized
paper made from pulps which have not been elemental chlorine
bleached. This pulp is from farmed sustainable forests and was
produced with special regard for the environment.
Throughout, the printing and binding have been planned to ensure
a sturdy, attractive publication which should give years of enjoyment.
If your copy fails to meet our high standards, please inform us and
we will gladly replace it.

Music Sales' complete catalogue describes thousands of titles and is
available in full colour sections by subject, direct from Music Sales
Limited. Please state your areas of interest and send a cheque/postal
order for £1.50 for postage to: Music Sales Limited, Newmarket Road,
Bury St. Edmunds, Suffolk IP33 3YB.

www.musicsales.com

Contents

BORN TO MAKE YOU HAPPY

Words & Music by Andreas Carlsson & Kristian Lundin

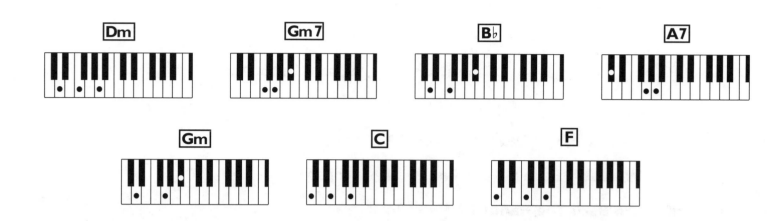

Voice: **Piano I**

Rhythm: **Club Pop**

Tempo: ♩ = **88**

I'm sit - tin' here a - lone up in my

room, and think - in' 'bout the times that we've been

through, oh my love. I'm look - ing at a pic - ture in my

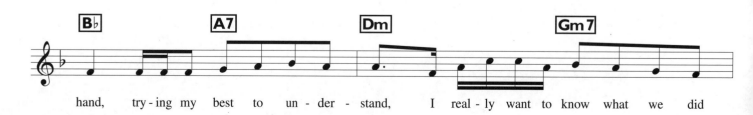

hand, try - ing my best to un - der - stand, I real - ly want to know what we did

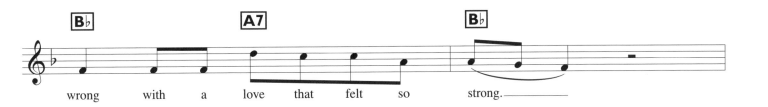

wrong with a love that felt so strong.

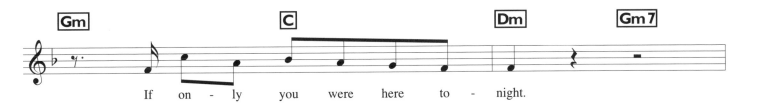

If on - ly you were here to - night.

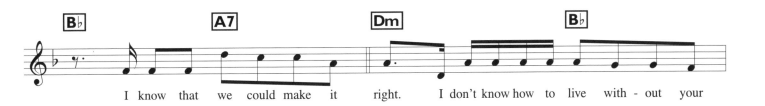

I know that we could make it right. I don't know how to live with - out your

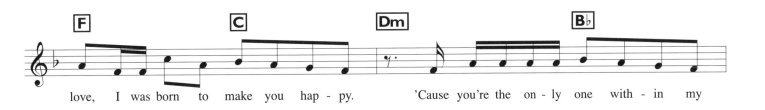

love, I was born to make you hap - py. 'Cause you're the on - ly one with - in my

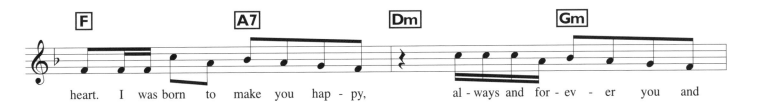

heart. I was born to make you hap - py, al - ways and for - ev - er you and

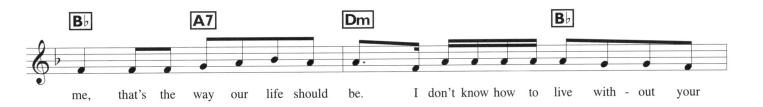

me, that's the way our life should be. I don't know how to live with - out your

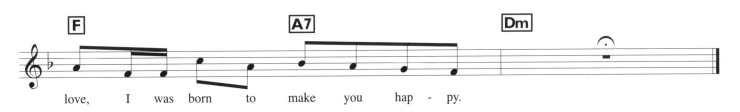

love, I was born to make you hap - py.

BRING IT ALL BACK

Words & Music by Eliot Kennedy, Mike Percy, Tim Lever & S Club 7

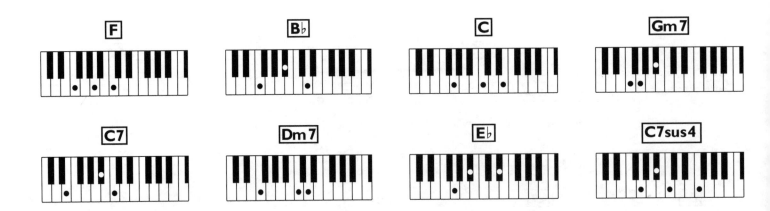

Voice: **Tenor Saxophone**

Rhythm: **Funky Pop 2**

Tempo: ♩ = 108

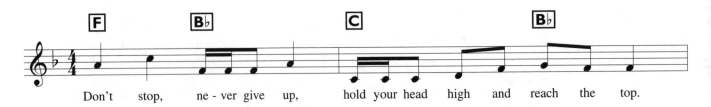

Don't stop, ne-ver give up, hold your head high and reach the top.

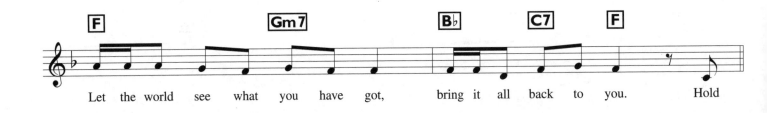

Let the world see what you have got, bring it all back to you. Hold

on to what— you try to be, your in-di-vi-du-a-li-ty. When the

world is on your shoul-ders, just smile and let it go. If

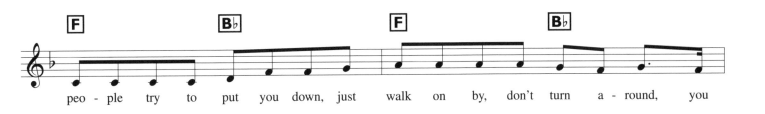

people try to put you down, just walk on by, don't turn a - round, you

on - ly have to ans - wer to your - self.   Don't you know it's   true   what they say,   in

life it ain't ea - sy,   but   your time's com - ing a - round.—   So don't you stop try - ing.

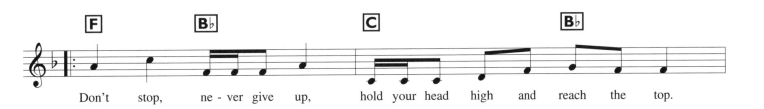

Don't   stop,   ne - ver give up,   hold your head   high   and   reach   the   top.

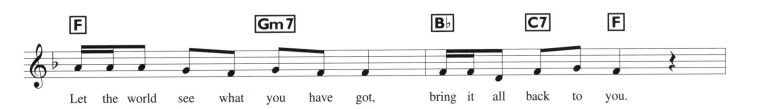

Let the world   see   what   you have got,   bring it all   back   to   you.

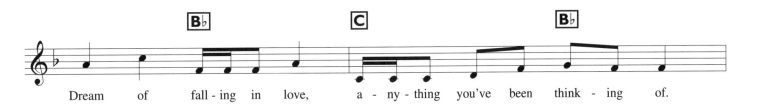

Dream   of   fall - ing in love,   a - ny - thing you've been think - ing   of.

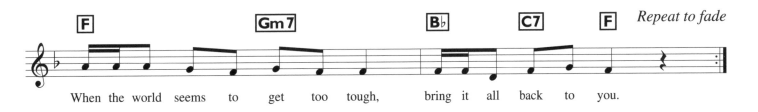

When the world   seems   to   get   too tough,   bring it all back to you.

CARNATION

Words & Music by Paul Weller

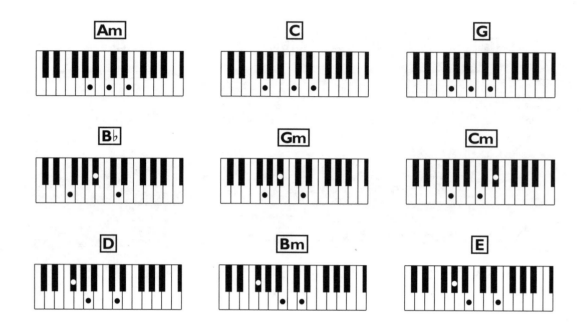

Voice: **Distortion Guitar**

Rhythm: **Pop Ballad**

Tempo: ♩ = 96

If you gave me a fresh__ car - na - tion, I would on - ly crush its

ten - der pe - tals. With me__ you have no__ es - cape,__ and at the same time there'll be

no-where to set - tle. I tram - ple down__ all life__ in my wake,__ I eat it up__

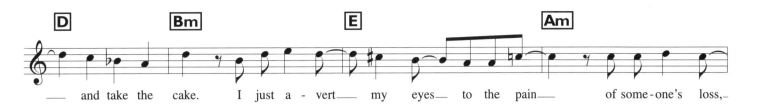

and take the cake. I just a-vert— my eyes— to the pain— of some-one's loss,—

— help-ing my gain. If you gave me a dream— for my pock - et,

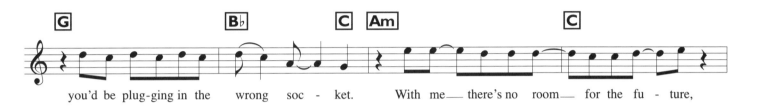

you'd be plug-ging in the wrong soc - ket. With me— there's no room— for the fu - ture,

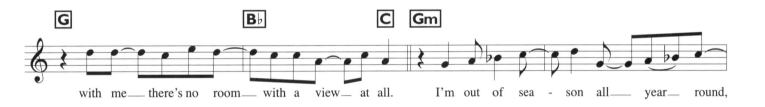

with me— there's no room— with a view— at all. I'm out of sea - son all— year— round,

— your ma-chi-ner-y roar— to my emp - ty sound. Touch my heart— and feel— win -

-ter, hold my hand— and be doomed for - ev-er. La la la— la la— la

Repeat to fade

la La la la— la la— la la La la la— la la— la

GO LET IT OUT

Words & Music by Noel Gallagher
© Copyright 2000 Oasis Music, Creation Songs Limited &
Sony/ATV Music Publishing (UK) Limited, 10 Great Marlborough Street, London W1.

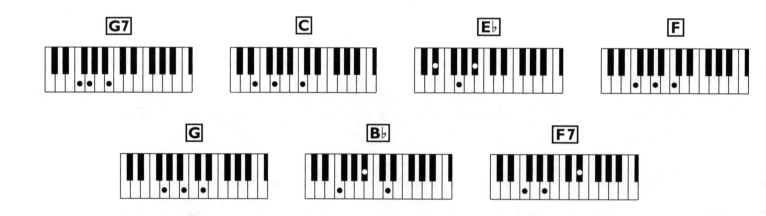

Voice: **Tenor Saxophone**

Rhythm: **Pop Rock 1**

Tempo: ♩ = 84

Paint no il - lu - sion, try to click with what— you got.

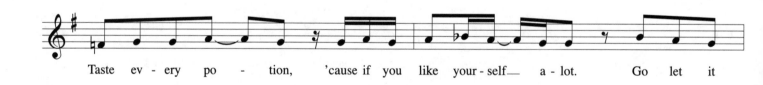

Taste ev - ery po - tion, 'cause if you like your - self— a - lot. Go let it

out, go let it in, and go let it out.

Life is pre - co - cious in the most pe - cu - liar way, sis - ter psy - cho - sis, don't

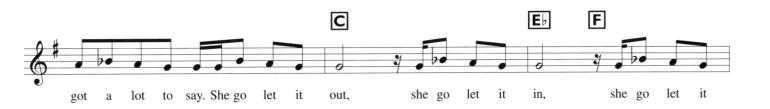

got a lot to say. She go let it out, she go let it in, she go let it

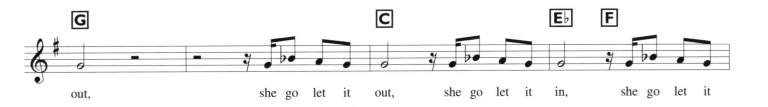

out, she go let it out, she go let it in, she go let it

out. Is it a - ny won - der why prin - ces and kings, —

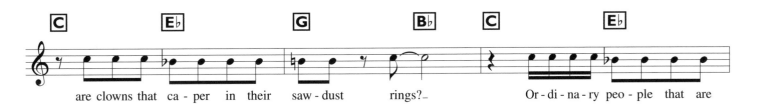

are clowns that ca - per in their saw - dust rings? — Or - di - na - ry peo - ple that are

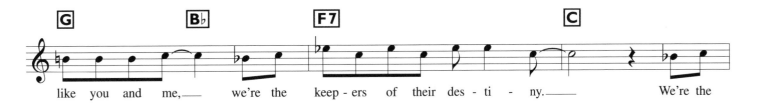

like you and me, — we're the keep - ers of their des - ti - ny. — We're the

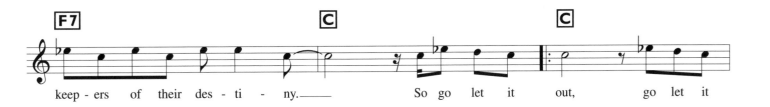

keep - ers of their des - ti - ny. — So go let it out, go let it

Repeat to fade

in, go let it out, don't let it in, and go let it

11

I HAVE A DREAM

Words & Music by Benny Andersson & Björn Ulvaeus

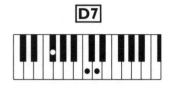
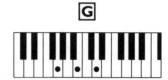
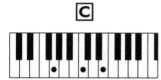

Voice: **Honky Tonk Piano**

Rhythm: **Pop Ballad**

Tempo: ♩ = 104

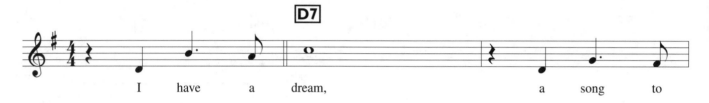

I have a dream, a song to

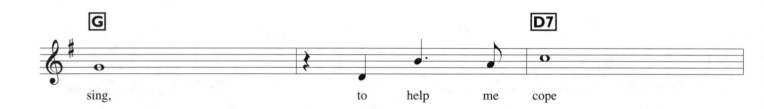

sing, to help me cope

with ev - 'ry - thing. If you see the

won - der of a fai - ry tale,

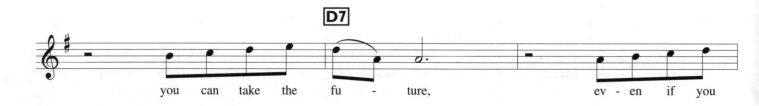

you can take the fu - ture, ev - en if you

fail.   I be - lieve in an - gels,

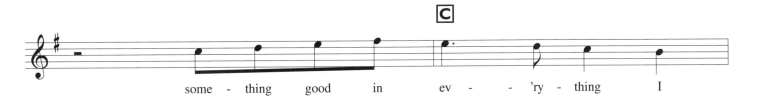

some - thing good in ev - - 'ry - thing I

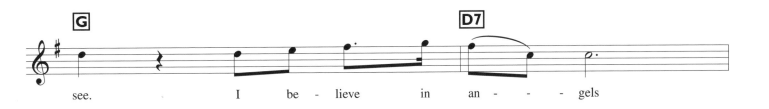

see.   I be - lieve in an - - - gels

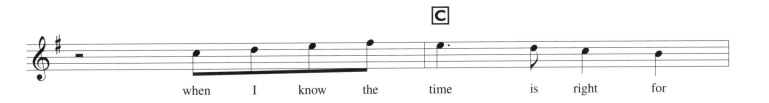

when I know the time is right for

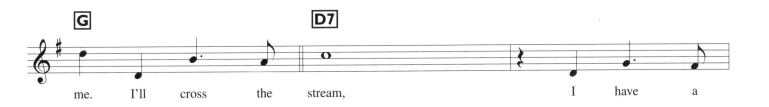

me. I'll cross the stream,   I have a

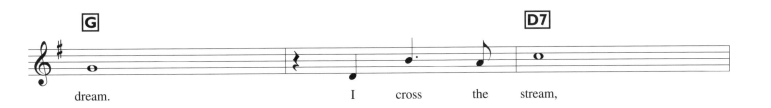

dream.   I cross the stream,

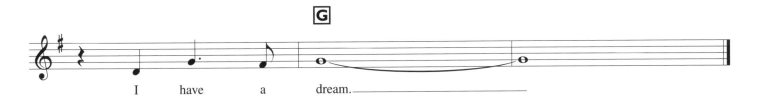

I have a dream.

I WOULDN'T BELIEVE YOUR RADIO

Words by Kelly Jones
Music by Kelly Jones, Richard Jones & Stuart Cable

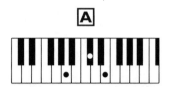 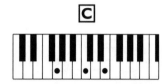 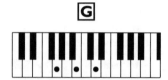 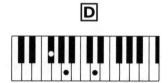

Voice: **Electric Guitar**

Rhythm: **Pop Ballad**

Tempo: ♩ = 124

Tra - vel - ling through_____ a

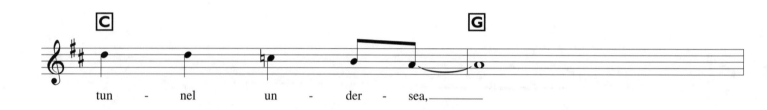

tun - nel un - der - sea,_____

you ne - ver know if it cracks in half,_____ you're

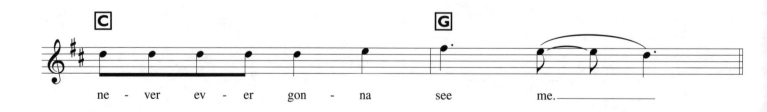

ne - ver ev - er gon - na see me._____

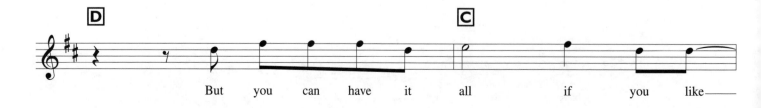

But you can have it all if you like_____

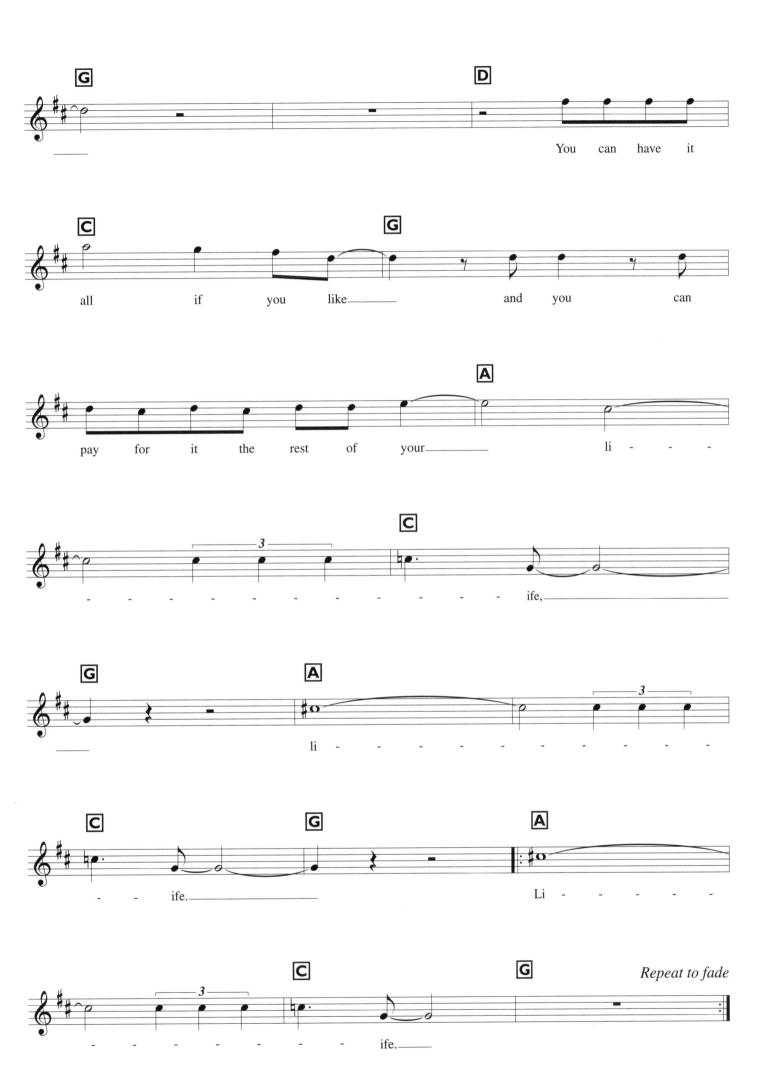

Repeat to fade

IF I COULD TURN BACK THE HANDS OF TIME

Words & Music by R. Kelly

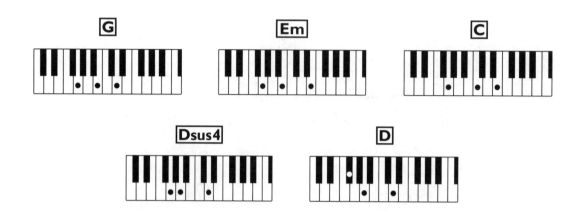

Voice: **Piano 1**

Rhythm: **Love Ballad**

Tempo: ♩. = 53

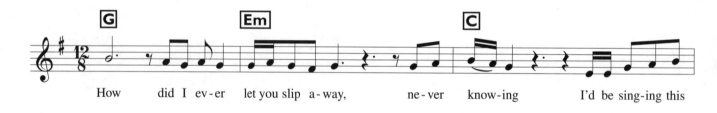

How did I ev-er let you slip a-way, ne-ver know-ing I'd be sing-ing this

song some day? And now I'm sink-ing,_____ sink-ing to rise no more,_____

ev-er since you_____ closed the door._____ If I could turn, turn back the

hands of time, then my dar-ling you'd_____ still be mine._____ If

16

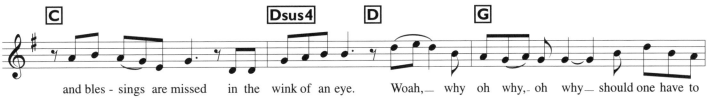

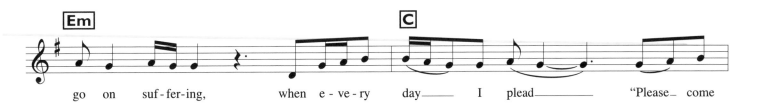

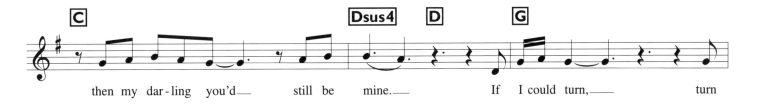

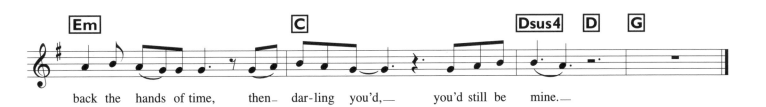

KEEP ON MOVIN'

Words & Music by Richard Stannard, Julian Gallagher, Richard Breen, Sean Conlon & Jason Brown

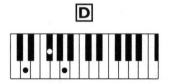
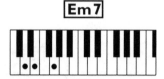

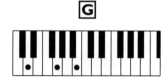

Voice: **Strings/Guitar Layer**

Rhythm: **Pop Rock 2**

Tempo: ♩ = 124

I woke up to-day with this feel - ing, that

bet - ter things are com - ing my way. And

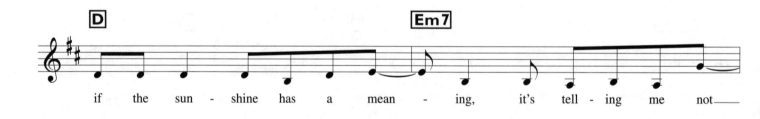

if the sun - shine has a mean - ing, it's tell - ing me not——

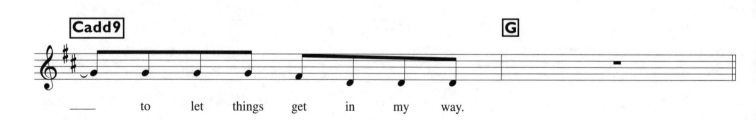

—— to let things get in my way.

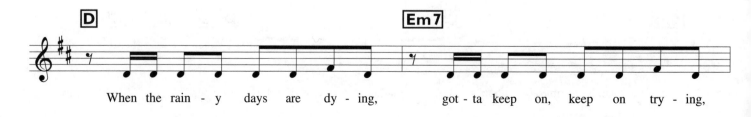

When the rain - y days are dy - ing, got - ta keep on, keep on try - ing,

all the bees and birds are fly - ing, ah.

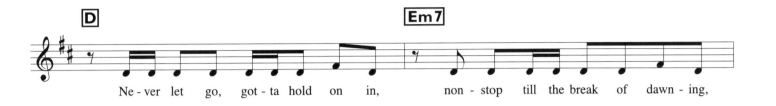

Ne - ver let go, got - ta hold on in, non - stop till the break of dawn - ing,

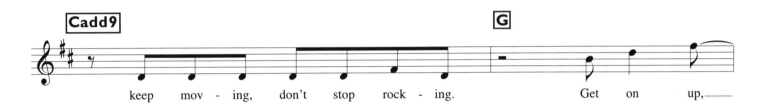

keep mov - ing, don't stop rock - ing. Get on up,

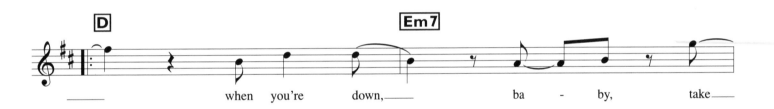

when you're down, ba - by, take

a good look a - round. I know it's not

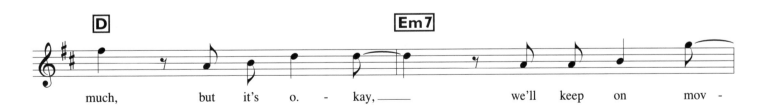

much, but it's o. - kay, we'll keep on mov -

Repeat to fade

- ing on a - ny - way. Get on up

19

LIFT ME UP

Words & Music by Geri Halliwell, Andy Watkins, Paul Wilson & Tracy Ackerman

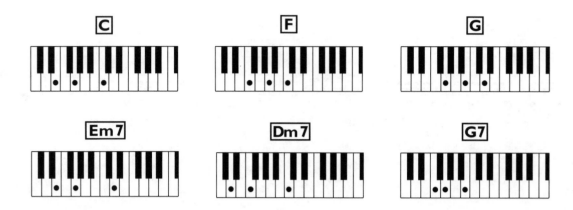

Voice: **Harp**

Rhythm: **New Age**

Tempo: ♩ = 108

Watch the first light___ kiss the new world,___

it's a won - der___ ba - by like you___ and I.

All the co - lours___ of the rain - bow___

go - ing some - where,___ ba - by like you___ and I.

LIVIN' LA VIDA LOCA

Words & Music by Desmond Child & Robi Rosa

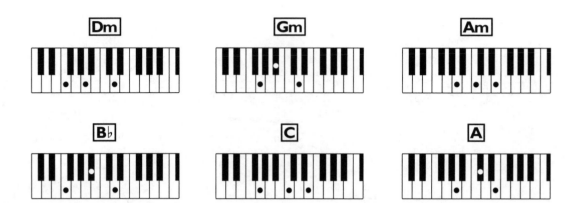

Voice: **Piano 2**

Rhythm: **Samba**

Tempo: ♩ = 88

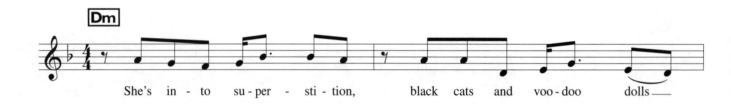

She's in-to su-per-sti-tion, black cats and voo-doo dolls

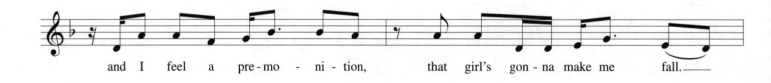

and I feel a pre-mo-ni-tion, that girl's gon-na make me fall.

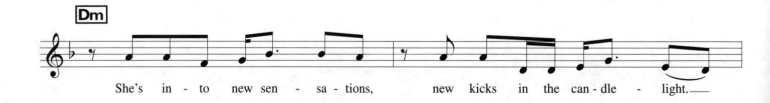

She's in-to new sen-sa-tions, new kicks in the can-dle-light.

She's got a new ad - dic - tion s'full ev - 'ry day and night. She'll make you take your clothes off and go

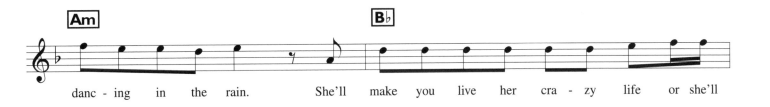

danc - ing in the rain. She'll make you live her cra - zy life or she'll

take a - way your pain like a bul - let to the brain.

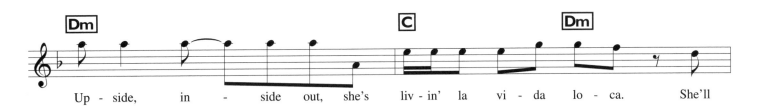

Up - side, in - side out, she's liv - in' la vi - da lo - ca. She'll

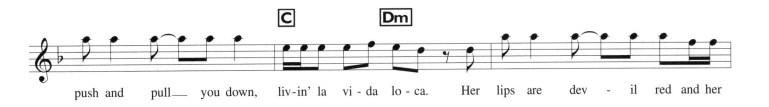

push and pull you down, liv - in' la vi - da lo - ca. Her lips are dev - il red and her

skin's the co - lour of mo - cha. She will wear you out, liv - in' la vi - da lo - ca,

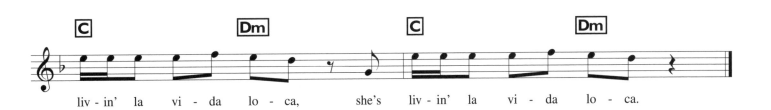

liv - in' la vi - da lo - ca, she's liv - in' la vi - da lo - ca.

MAMBO No.5 (A LITTLE BIT OF...)

Music by Perez 'Prez' Prado
Words by Lou Bega & Zippy

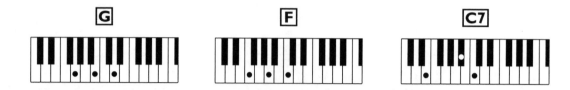

Voice: **Trumpet**

Rhythm: **Swing**

Tempo: ♩ = 172

One, two, three four five,— ev-'ry-bo-dy in the car, so come

on let's ride— to the li-quor store a-round the cor-ner. The boys say they

want some gin and juice but I real-ly don't want a beer bust like I

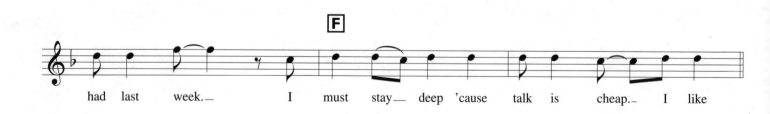

had last week.— I must stay— deep 'cause talk is cheap.— I like

Mo-ni-ca in my life,— a lit-tle bit of E-ri-ca by my side,—

EASIEST KEYBOARD COLLECTION

The Easiest Keyboard Books Ever!

Start playing all your favourite music today
with this great series of easy-play books
for electronic keyboard

Hundreds of chart hits, ballads, love songs, film & TV themes,
showstoppers, jazz & blues standards, popular classics and more...

EASIEST KEYBOARD COLLECTION

It's So Easy...

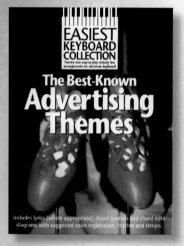

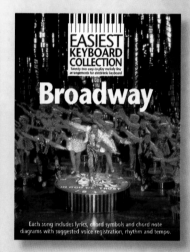

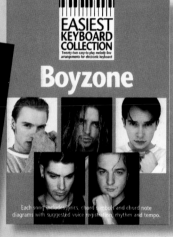

Abba
Includes:
Chiquitita
Dancing Queen
Fernando
Take A Chance On Me
Order No. AM959860

Ballads
Includes:
Autumn Leaves
For The Good Times
Green, Green Grass Of Home
This Guy's In Love With You
Order No. AM952116

The Beatles
Includes:
Can't Buy Me Love
Eleanor Rigby
Lady Madonna
Yesterday
Order No. NO90686

The Best-Known Advertising Themes
Includes:
Female Of The Species (Impulse)
Flower Duet from Delibes' Lakmé
  (British Airways)
Guaglione (Guinness)
Marvellous (Renault Megane Scenic)
Order No. AM956550

The Best Party Hits
Includes:
Dizzy
Oops Upside Your Head
Saturday Night
Y.M.C.A.
Order No. AM955812

Boyzone
Includes:
A Different Beat
Father And Son
Love Me For A Reason
No Matter What
Order No. AM958331

Broadway
Includes:
Big Spender (Sweet Charity)
Empty Chairs At Empty Tables
  (Les Misérables)
Tonight (West Side Story)
What I Did For Love
  (A Chorus Line)
Order No. AM952127

Celine Dion
Includes:
Falling Into You
My Heart Will Go On
The Power Of Love
Think Twice
Order No. AM959850

Chart Hits
Includes:
Barbie Girl (Aqua)
I Believe I Can Fly (R. Kelly)
Picture Of You (Boyzone)
You Must Love Me (Madonna)
Order No. AM952083

Christmas
Includes:
Frosty The Snowman
Mary's Boy Child
Silent Night
Winter Wonderland
Order No. AM952105

Classic Blues
Includes;
Basin Street Blues
Crazy
Georgia On My Mind
Memphis Blues
Order No. AM950697

Classics
Includes:
Air On The 'G' String
  (J.S. Bach)
Eine Kleine Nachtmusik -
  Themes (Mozart)
Ode To Joy from
  Symphony No.9 (Beethoven)
Swan Lake - Theme
  (Tchaikovsky)
Order No. AM952094

The Corrs
Includes:
Dreams
So Young
Someday
What Can I Do
Order No. AM959849

Disco Classics
Includes:
Disco Inferno (Trammps)
I Will Survive (Gloria Gaynor)
Night Fever (The Bee Gees)
Rasputin (Boney M)
Order No. AM959035

Can't read chord symbols? No problem...
Easy-to-follow keyboard diagrams are grouped together at the start of each piece
and show all the left-hand chord voicings used... it really couldn't be easier.

All the books in this great series contain 22 easy-to-play melody line arrangements, with no page turns to distract your concentration!

Suggested voice registration, automatic rhythm and tempo are given at the start of each piece and left-hand chord symbols with lyrics (where appropriate) are included with the music.

Elton John
Includes:
Candle In The Wind
Circle Of Life
Daniel
Song For Guy
Order No. AM958320

Film Themes
Includes:
A Whole New World (Aladdin)
Circle Of Life (The Lion King)
Love Is All Around
   (Four Weddings And A Funeral)
Speak Softly Love (The Godfather)
Order No. AM952050

Hits Of The 90s
Includes:
A Design For Life
   (Manic Street Preachers)
Ironic (Alanis Morissette)
Never Ever (All Saints)
Viva Forever (Spice Girls)
Order No. AM955780

Jazz Classics
Includes:
Don't Dream Of Anybody
   But Me (Li'l Darlin')
Fly Me To The Moon
Honeysuckle Rose
I'm Beginning To See The Light
Order No. AM952061

Love Songs
Includes:
Just The Two Of Us
Take My Breath Away
The Wind Beneath My Wings
Up Where We Belong
Order No. AM950708

Pop Classics
Includes:
A Whiter Shade Of Pale
   (Procol Harum)
Bridge Over Troubled Water
   (Simon & Garfunkel)
Hey Jude (The Beatles)
Massachusetts (The Bee Gees)
Order No. AM944196

Pop Hits
Includes:
Country House (Blur)
Money For Nothing (Dire Straits)
Rotterdam (Beautiful South)
Wonderful Tonight (Eric Clapton)
Order No. AM952072

Showstoppers
includes:
Consider Yourself (Oliver!)
Do You Hear The People Sing?
   (Les Misérables)
I Know Him So Well (Chess)
Maria (West Side Story)
Order No. AM944218

Sports Themes
Includes:
La Copa de la Vida (World Cup '98)
Nessun Dorma from Turandot
   (BBC World Cup '90)
Sporting Occasion
   (Wimbledon Closing Theme)
You'll Never Walk Alone
   (Football Anthem)
Order No. AM955801

Swing
Includes:
I Wan'na Be Like You
Lazy River
Moonlight Serenade
Take The 'A' Train
Order No. AM959101

TV Themes
Includes:
Casualty
EastEnders
Red Dwarf
The Black Adder
Order No. AM944207

60s Hits
Includes:
House Of The Rising Sun
   (The Animals)
Let's Dance (Chris Montez)
Only The Lonely (Roy Orbison)
Young Girl
   (Gary Puckett & Union Gap)
Order No. AM955768

80s Hits
Includes:
A Woman In Love (Barbra Streisand)
Eternal Flame (The Bangles)
Private Dancer (Tina Turner)
Who's That Girl? (Eurythmics)
Order No. AM955779

90s Hits
Includes:
Always (Bon Jovi)
Fields Of Gold (Sting)
When You Tell Me That
   You Love Me (Diana Ross)
Wonderwall (Oasis)
Order No. AM944229

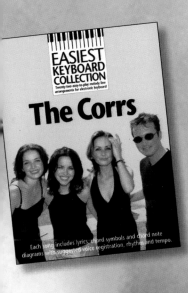

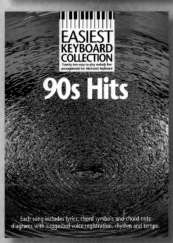

...Start Playing Right Away!

EASIEST KEYBOARD COLLECTION

Sample The Whole Series
With These Special Pop Selections...

a lit-tle bit of Ri-ta's all I need,___ a lit-tle bit of

Ti-na's what I see.___ A lit-tle bit of San-dra in the sun,___

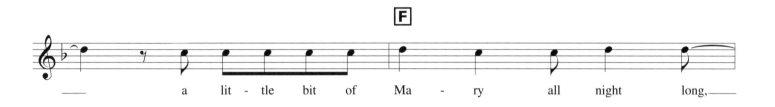
a lit-tle bit of Ma-ry all night long,___

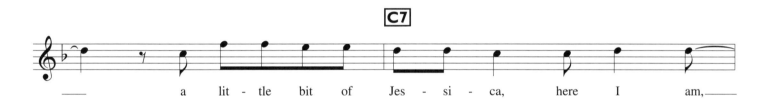
a lit-tle bit of Jes-si-ca, here I am,___

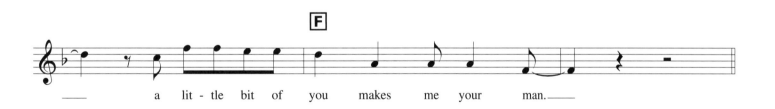
a lit-tle bit of you makes me your man.___

MAN! I FEEL LIKE A WOMAN!

Words & Music by Shania Twain & R.J. Lange

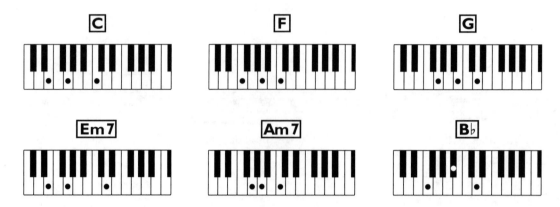

Voice: **Electric Guitar**

Rhythm: **Chicago Blues**

Tempo: ♩ = 120

I'm go - ing out to - night, I'm feel - ing al - right, gon -

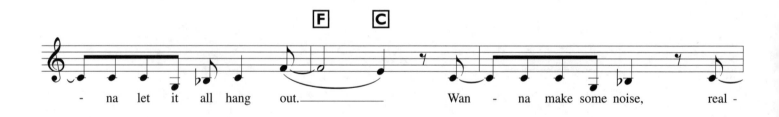

- na let it all hang out. _____ Wan - na make some noise, real -

- ly raise my voice, yeah, _____ I wan - na scream and shout. _____

Oh— oh oh,— go to-tal-ly cra - zy,— for-get I'm a la - dy,—

men's shirts, short skirts. Oh— oh oh,— real - ly go wild, yeah,—

do - ing it in style.— Oh— oh oh,— get in the ac - tion,—

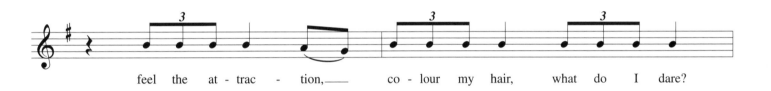

feel the at - trac - tion,— co - lour my hair, what do I dare?

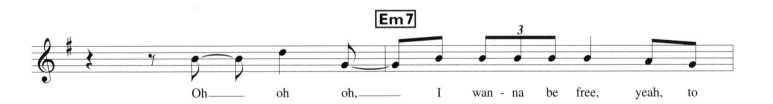

Oh— oh oh,— I wan - na be free, yeah, to

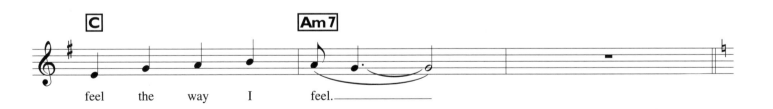

feel the way I feel.—

I feel like a wo - man.

PERFECT MOMENT

Words & Music by James Marr & Wendy Page

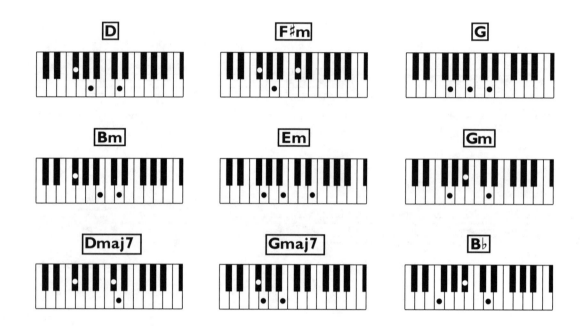

Voice: **Electric Guitar 2**

Rhythm: **Pop Ballad**

Tempo: ♩ = 68

This is my mo-ment, this is my per-fect mo-ment with you.

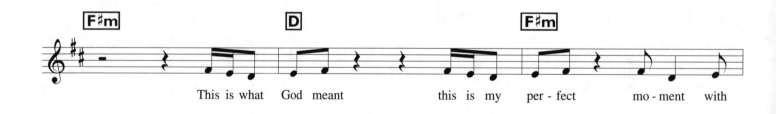

This is what God meant this is my per-fect mo-ment with

you. Wish I could freeze this space in

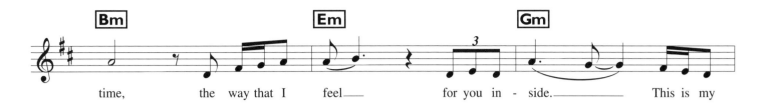

time,   the way that I   feel___   for you in - side.___   This is my

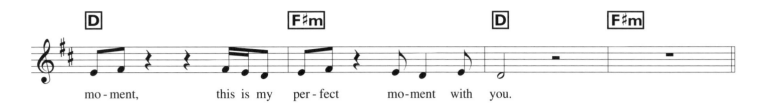

mo - ment,   this is my   per - fect   mo - ment with   you.

Tell   me you love me,   the   mo - ment you leave,   you're more than a sha - dow,

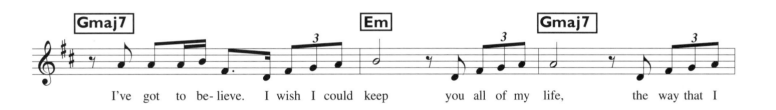

I've got   to be- lieve.   I wish I could keep   you all of my life,   the way that I

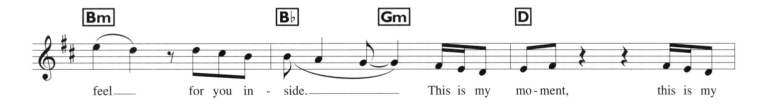

feel___   for you in - side.___   This is my   mo - ment,   this is my

per - fect   mo - ment with   you.   This is my   mo - ment,___   this is

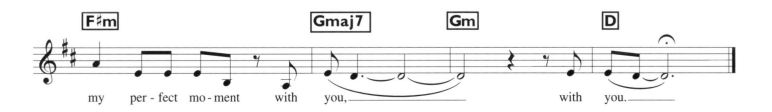

my   per - fect mo - ment with   you,___   with   you.___

PRAISE YOU

Words & Music by Norman Cook & Camille Yarborough
© Copyright 1998 Maat Music Company, Vogue Music & PolyGram Music Publishing Limited.
Universal Music Publishing Limited, 77 Fulham Palace Road, London W6

RADIO

Words & Music by Andrea Corr, Caroline Corr, Sharon Corr & Jim Corr

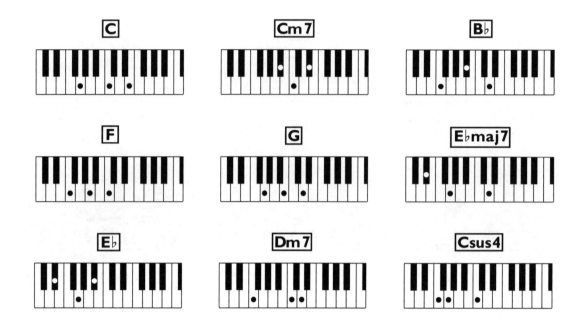

Voice: **Piano 1**

Rhythm: **Pop Rock 1**

Tempo: ♩= 108

It's late at night and I'm feel-ing down, there are

cou-ples stand-ing on the street shar-in' sum-mer kis-ses and sil-ly sounds.___

So I step in-side, pour a

glass of wine, with a full glass and an emp-ty heart, I search for some-thing to oc-cu-py my

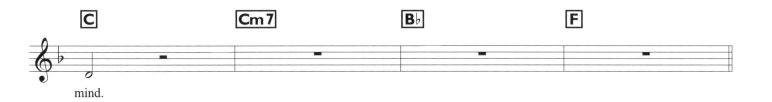

mind.

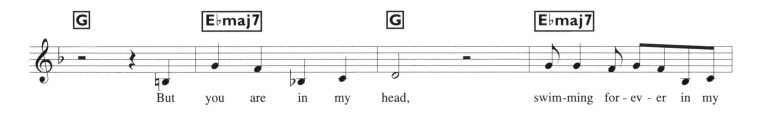

But you are in my head, swim-ming for-ev-er in my

head, tang-led in my dreams, swim-ming for-ev-er.

So I lis-ten to the ra-di-o, and all the songs we

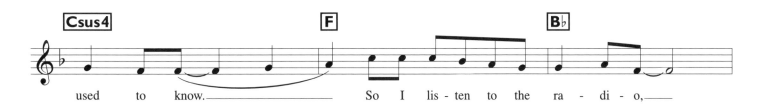

used to know. So I lis-ten to the ra-di-o,

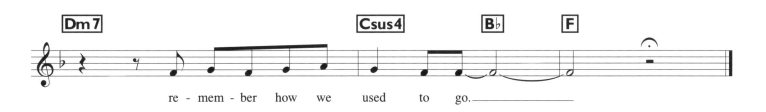

re-mem-ber how we used to go.

RISE

Words & Music by Bob Dylan, Gabrielle,
Ferdy Unger-Hamilton & Ollie Dagois
© Copyright 1999 Ram's Horn Music, USA (50%)/
Perfect Songs Limited, The Blue Building, 42-46 St. Luke's Mews,
London W11 (33.33%)/Copyright Control (16.67%).
All Rights Reserved. International Copyright Secured.

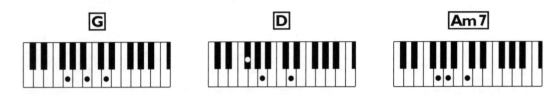

Voice: **Clarinet**

Rhythm: **Soul Ballad**

Tempo: ♩ = 72

Mm_____ Mm_____

__ I know that it's ov - er,_____

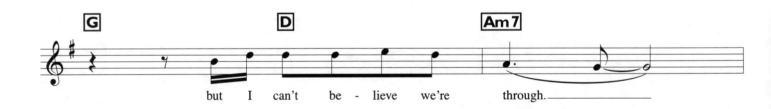

but I can't be - lieve we're through._____

They say____ that time's a heal - er,____ yeah,

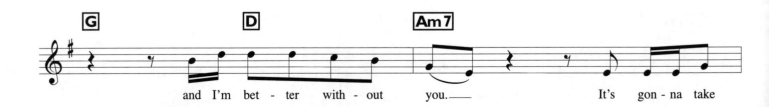

and I'm bet - ter with - out you.____ It's gon - na take

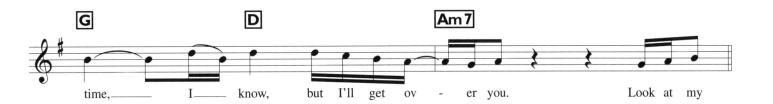
time,___ I ___ know, but I'll get ov - er you. Look at my

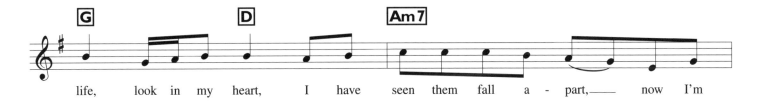
life, look in my heart, I have seen them fall a - part,___ now I'm

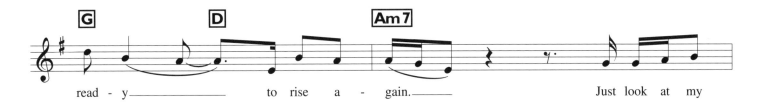
read - y_____ to rise a - gain.___ Just look at my

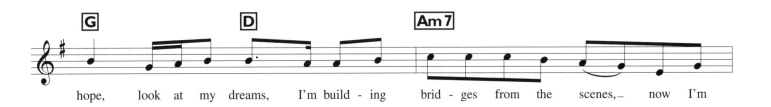
hope, look at my dreams, I'm build - ing brid - ges from the scenes,_ now I'm

read - y_____ to rise a - gain.___ I'm gon - na make it al -

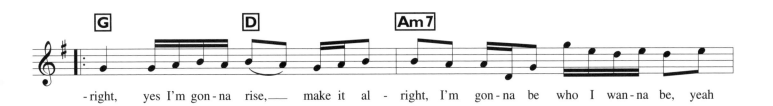
- right, yes I'm gon - na rise,___ make it al - right, I'm gon - na be who I wan - na be, yeah

Repeat to fade

ba - by, yeah___ yeah._____ I'm gon - na make it al -

SAY YOU'LL BE MINE

Words & Music by Andrew Frampton & Pete Waterman
© Copyright 1998 All Boys Music Limited/BMG Music Publishing Limited,
Bedford House, 69-79 Fulham High Street, London SW6 (50%)/
EMI Music Publishing Limited, 127 Charing Cross Road, London WC2 (50%).
This arrangement © Copyright 2000 BMG Music Publishing Limited for their share of interest.
All Rights Reserved. International Copyright Secured.

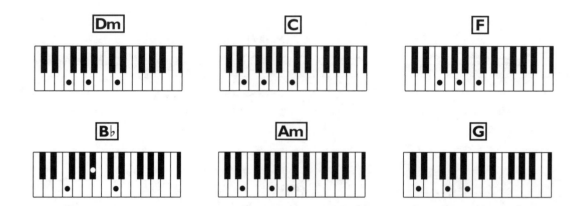

Voice: **Electric Piano 3**

Rhythm: **Straight Rock**

Tempo: ♩= 100

Ba-by I was hyp-no-tised when I looked in-to your eyes, saw the love I'd been wait-

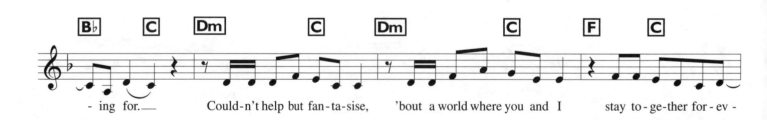

-ing for.— Could-n't help but fan-ta-sise, 'bout a world where you and I stay to-ge-ther for-ev-

-er-more. Don't he-si-tate,— 'cause I can't con-trol— my feel-ings, just can't wait,— now I

know where this— is lead-in'. Ba-by please,— this heart's on the line,— don't waste this pre-cious time,—

SHE'S THE ONE

Words & Music by Karl Wallinger

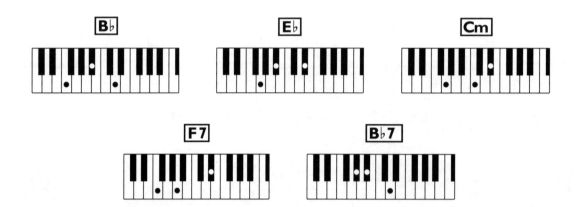

Voice: **Syntehsizer Lead 2**

Rhythm: **Pop Rock I**

Tempo: ♩ = 78

I was her,____ she was me,____ we were one,____

____ we were free,____ and if there's some-bo-dy call-ing me on,____

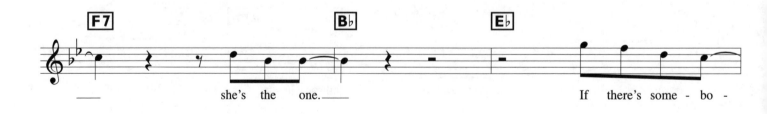

____ she's the one.____ If there's some-bo-

-dy call-ing me on,____ she's the one.____

When you get to where you wan-na go,___ and you know the things you wan-na know,___ you're

smil - - - ing. When you said what you wan-na say___ and you

know the way you wan-na play,___ yeah, you'll be so high, you'll be fly - - -

- ing. I was her,___ she was me,___ we were one,___ we were free.

___ And if there's some-bo - dy call-ing me on,___ she's the one,___

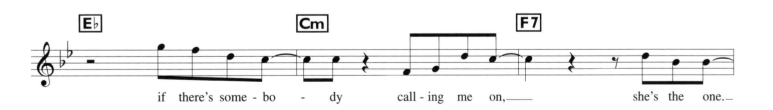

if there's some-bo - dy call-ing me on,___ she's the one.___

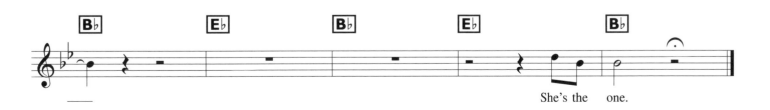

___ She's the one.

SING IT BACK

Words & Music by Mark Brydon & Roisin Murphy

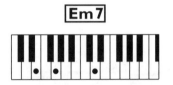
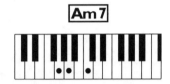
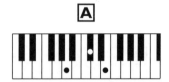
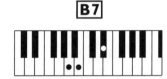

Voice: **Bass/Gut Guitar Split**

Rhythm: **Club Pop**

Tempo: ♩ = 124

When you are rea - dy, I will sur - ren - der, take me and do as you

wish. Have what you want, your way's al - ways the best way.

I have suc - cumbed to this pas - sive sen - sa - tion,

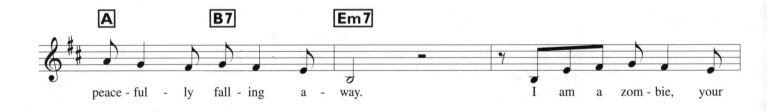

peace - ful - ly fall - ing a - way. I am a zom - bie, your

wish will com - mand me, laugh as I fall to my knees.

Bring it back, sing it back, bring it back,

sing it back to me.___ Bring it back, sing it back,

bring it back, sing it back to me.___ Come, come,

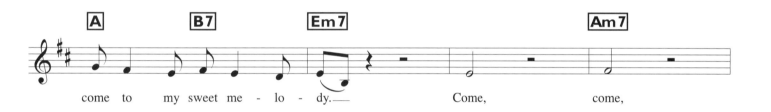

come to my sweet me - lo - dy.___ Come, come,

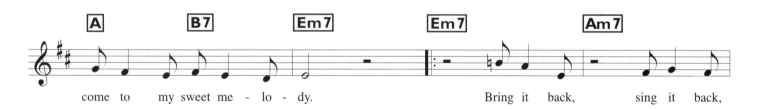

come to my sweet me - lo - dy. Bring it back, sing it back,

bring it back, sing it back to me.___ Bring it back,

Repeat to fade

sing it back, bring it back, sing it back to me.___

THAT'S THE WAY IT IS

Words & Music by Max Martin, Kristian Lundin & Andreas Carlsson
© Copyright 1999 Grantsville Publishing Limited, administered by
Zomba Music Publishers Limited, 165-167 High Road, London NW10.
All Rights Reserved. International Copyright Secured.

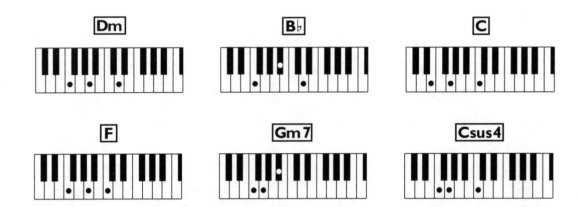

Voice: **Flute**

Rhythm: **Soft Rock 3**

Tempo: ♩ = 92

I can read your mind,— and I know your sto - ry, I

see what you're go - ing through,— yeah.—— It's an up - hill climb,— and I'm

feel - ing sor - ry, but I know it will come to you,——

—— yeah.— Don't sur - ren - der,— 'cause you can win— in this

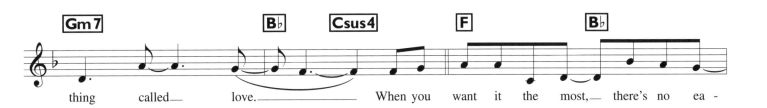

thing called— love.— When you want it the most,— there's no ea-

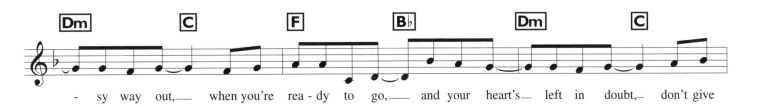

-sy way out,— when you're rea-dy to go,— and your heart's— left in doubt,— don't give

up on your faith,— love— comes to those— who be-lieve— it,—

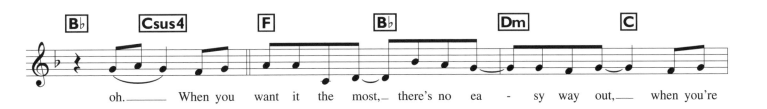

oh.— When you want it the most,— there's no ea-sy way out,— when you're

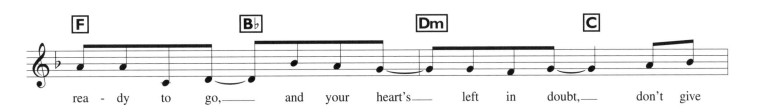

rea-dy to go,— and your heart's— left in doubt,— don't give

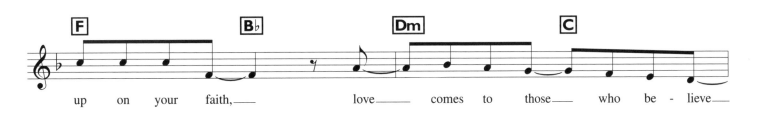

up on your faith,— love— comes to those— who be-lieve—

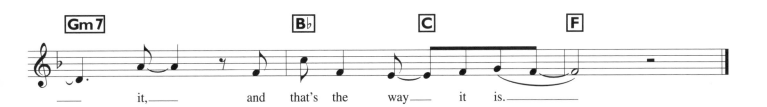

— it,— and that's the way— it is.—

TURN

Words & Music by Fran Healy
© Copyright 1999 Sony/ATV Music Publishing (UK) Limited,
10 Great Marlborough Street, London W1.
All Rights Reserved. International Copyright Secured.

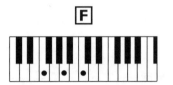
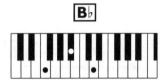
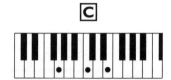
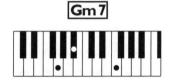

Voice: **Distortion Guitar**

Rhythm: **Straight Rock**

Tempo: ♩ = 74

I want to see what peo - ple saw,

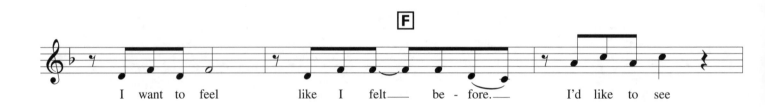

I want to feel like I felt be - fore. I'd like to see

the king - dom come, I want to feel for - ev - er young.

I want to sing, to sing my song.

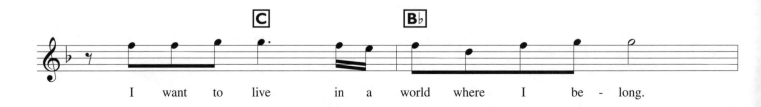

I want to live in a world where I be - long.

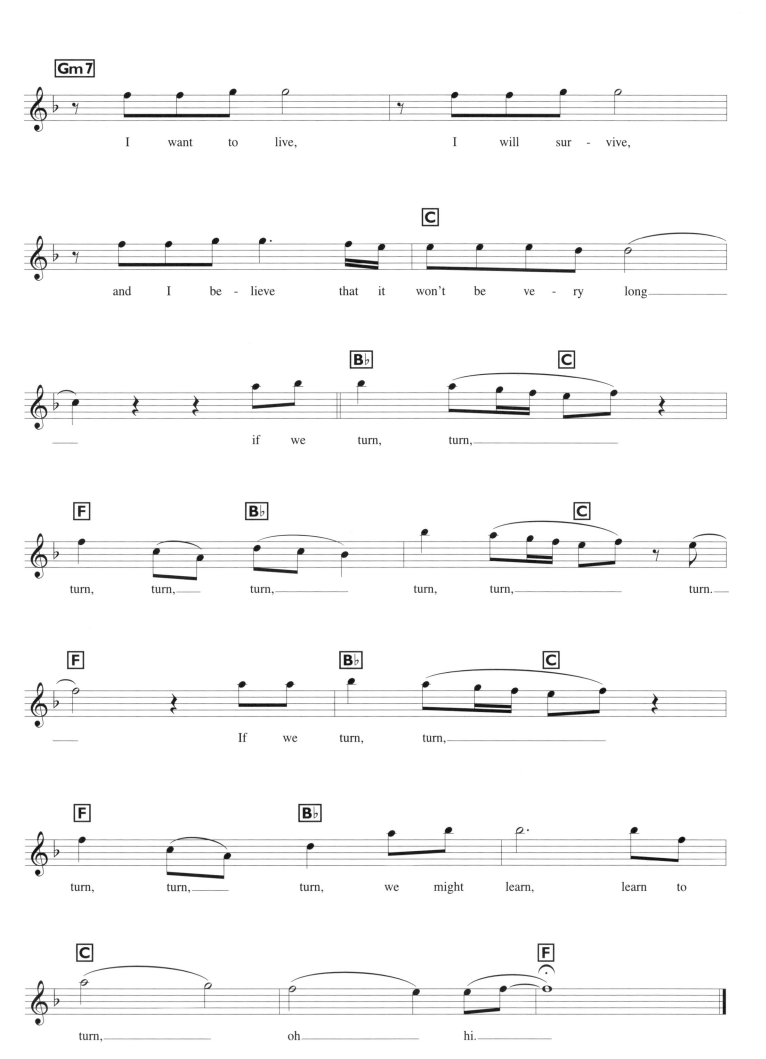

WHEN YOU SAY NOTHING AT ALL

Words & Music by Paul Overstreet & Don Schlitz

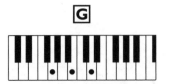 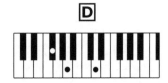 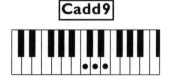 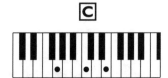

Voice: **Electric Piano 2**

Rhythm: **Pop Ballad**

Tempo: ♩ = 88

It's a - maz - ing how you can speak right____ to my heart____

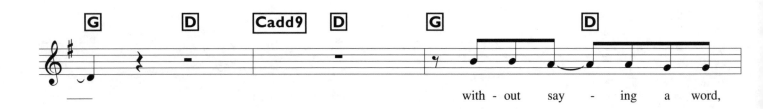

____ with - out say - ing a word,

you can light up the dark.____

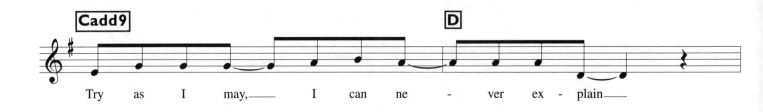

Try as I may,____ I can ne - ver ex - plain____

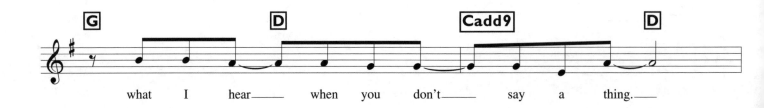

what I hear____ when you don't____ say a thing.____

The smile on your face___ lets me know___

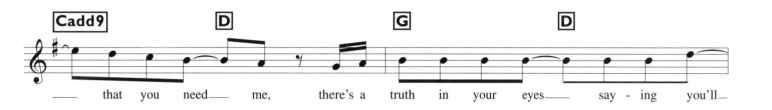
___ that you need___ me, there's a truth in your eyes___ say - ing you'll___

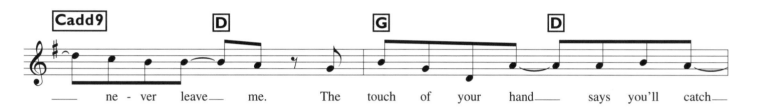
___ ne - ver leave___ me. The touch of your hand___ says you'll catch___

___ me wher - ev - er I fall.___

You say it best,___ when you say no - thing at all.___

Repeat to fade

You say it best___ when you say no - thing at all.___

EASIEST KEYBOARD COLLECTION

Easy-to-play melody line arrangements for all keyboards with chord symbols and lyrics. Suggested registration, rhythm and tempo are included for each song together with keyboard diagrams showing left-hand chord voicings used.

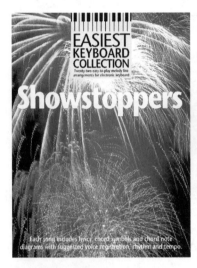

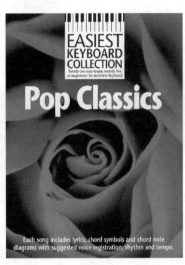

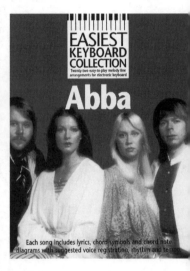

Showstoppers

Consider Yourself (Oliver!), Do You Hear The People Sing? (Les Misérables), I Know Him So Well (Chess), Maria (West Side Story), Smoke Gets In Your Eyes (Roberta) and 17 more big stage hits.
Order No. AM944218

Pop Classics

A Whiter Shade Of Pale (Procol Harum), Bridge Over Troubled Water (Simon & Garfunkel), Crocodile Rock (Elton John) and 19 more classic hit songs, including Hey Jude (The Beatles), Imagine (John Lennon), and Massachusetts (The Bee Gees).
Order No. AM944196

90s Hits

Over 20 of the greatest hits of the 1990s, including Always (Bon Jovi), Fields Of Gold (Sting), Have I Told You Lately (Rod Stewart), One Sweet Day (Mariah Carey), Say You'll Be There (Spice Girls), and Wonderwall (Oasis).
Order No. AM944229

Abba

A great collection of 22 Abba hit songs. Includes: Dancing Queen, Fernando, I Have A Dream, Mamma Mia, Super Trouper, Take A Chance On Me, Thank You For The Music, The Winner Takes It All, and Waterloo.
Order No. AM959860

Also available...

Ballads, Order No. AM952116
The Beatles, Order No. NO90686
Boyzone, Order No. AM958331
Broadway, Order No. AM952127
Celine Dion, Order No. AM959850
Chart Hits, Order No. AM952083
Christmas, Order No. AM952105
Classic Blues, Order No. AM950697
Classics, Order No. AM952094

The Corrs, Order No. AM959849
Elton John, Order No. AM958320
Film Themes, Order No. AM952050
Hits of the 90s, Order No. AM955780
Jazz Classics, Order No. AM952061
Love Songs, Order No. AM950708
Pop Hits, Order No. AM952072
60s Hits, Order No. AM955768
80s Hits, Order No. AM955779

...plus many more!